D1560591

THIS BOOK IS DEDICATED TO MY DEAR GRANDPA

I ♥ Y

_____

THANK YOU SO MUCH
YOU'RE ALWAYS WITH ME!

MY AMAZING GRANDPA

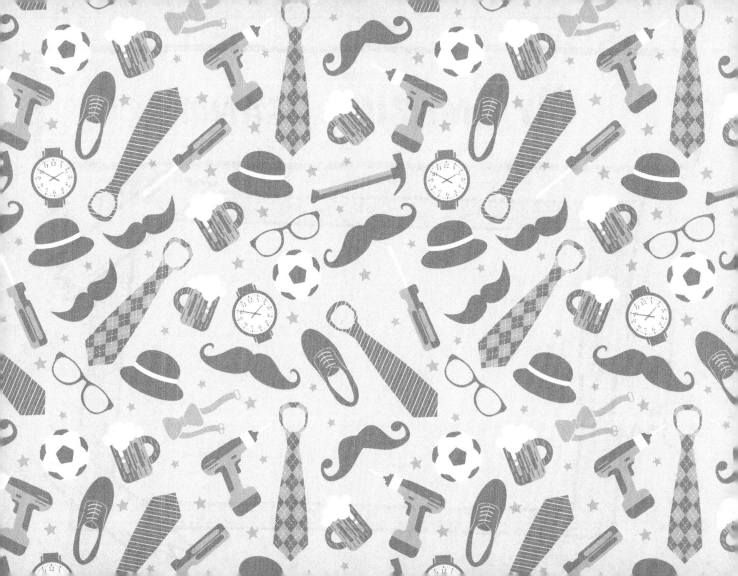

My Grandpa's name is _____,

He's _____ old. Dad has

_____ eyes and _____ hair.

His favorite color is _____

His favorite food is _____

My Grandpa's favorite music is

_____

He always listens to it when

_____

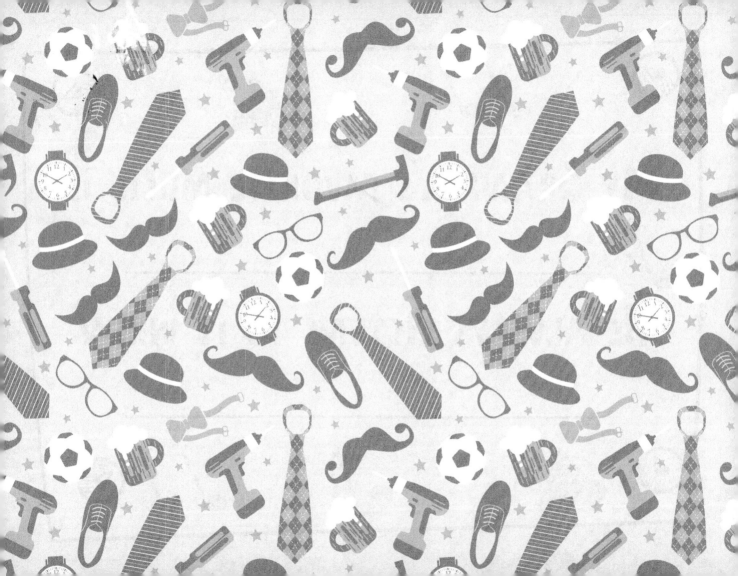

WHEN I GROW UP
I HOPE TO BE
WITH MY GRANDPA

_____

_____

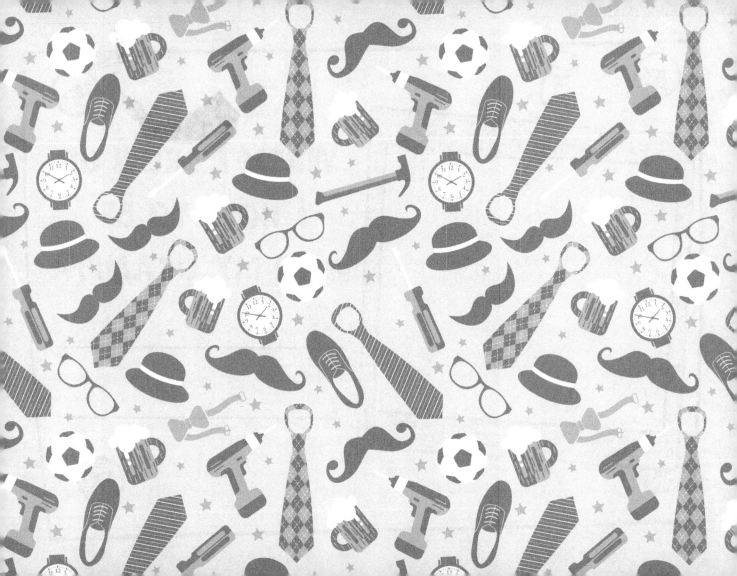

MY GRANDPA MAKES ME LAUGH WHEN

_____

_____

_____

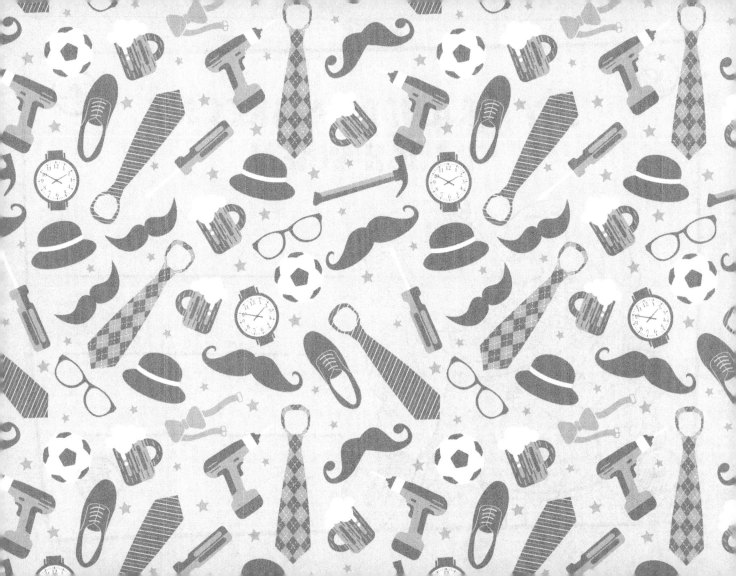

MY GRANDPA'S BEST FRIENDS

I WILL ALWAYS BE GRATEFUL TO HIM FOR HELPING ME WITH

1.

_____

_____

2.

_____

_____

3.

_____

_____

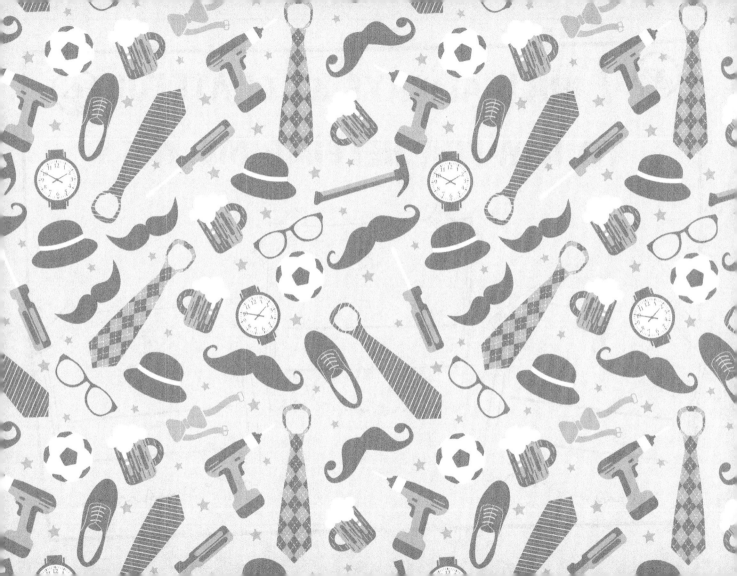

GRANDPA WORKS AT

_____

_____

HE'S OVER THERE

_____

_____

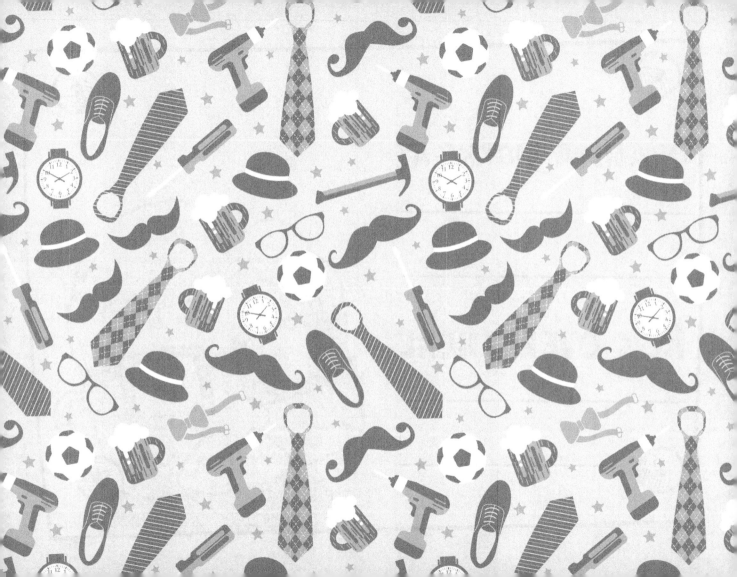

I HAVE VERY FOND MEMORIES OF THE TRIP WITH MY GRANDPA TO

_____

WE WERE THERE

_____

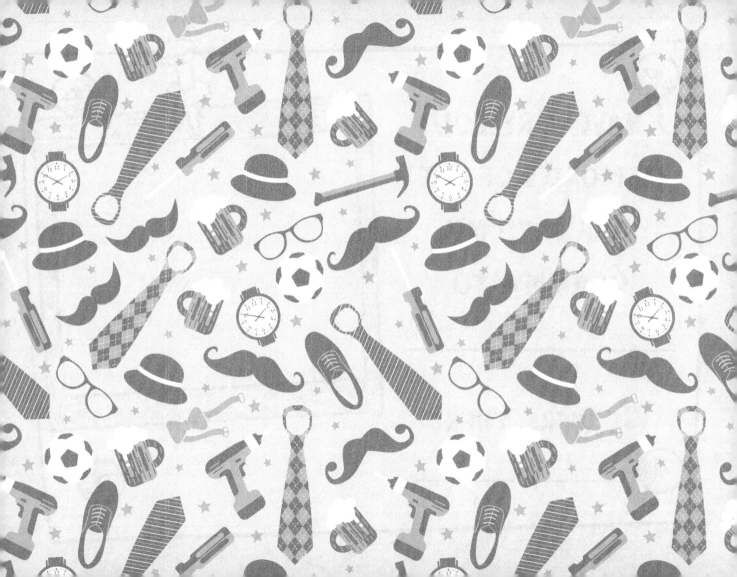

THE GREATEST THING MY SUPER GRANDPA HAS

- _____
- _____
- _____
- _____

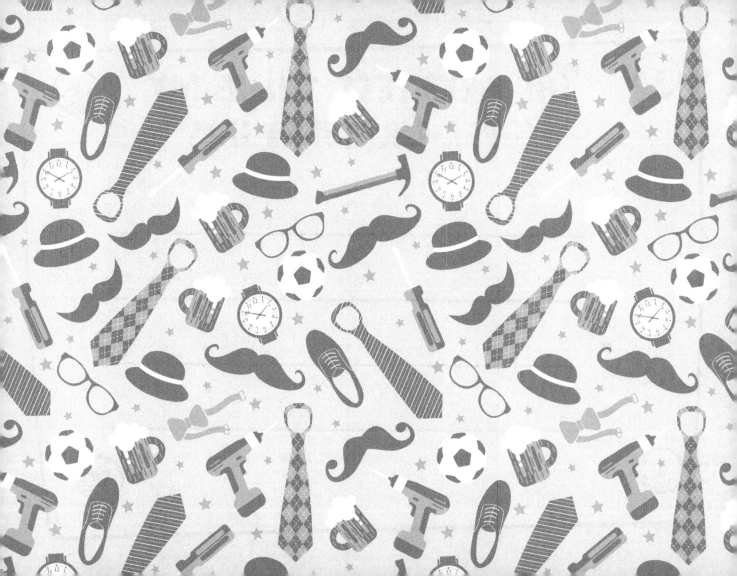

MY WONDERFUL GRANDPA'S HOBBY is

_____

_____

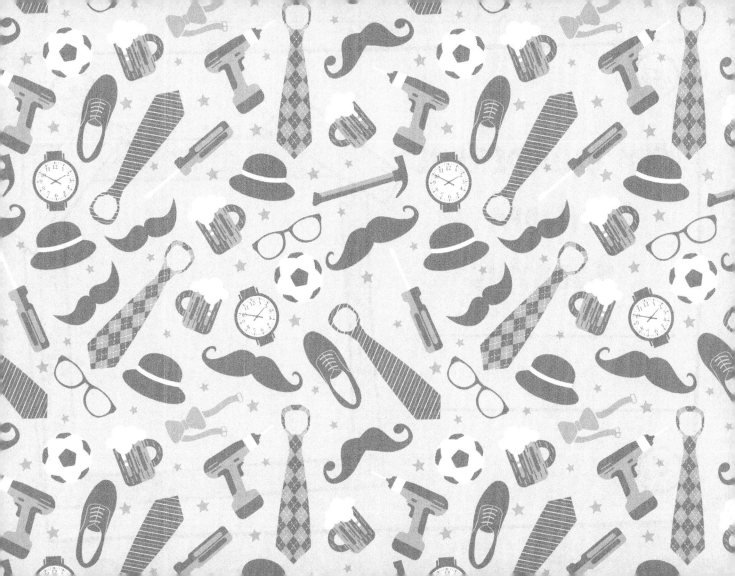

WHEN WE REST, WE LIKE THE MOST:

1. _____

2. _____

3. _____

I WOULD LIKE MY GRANDPA TO TEACH ME

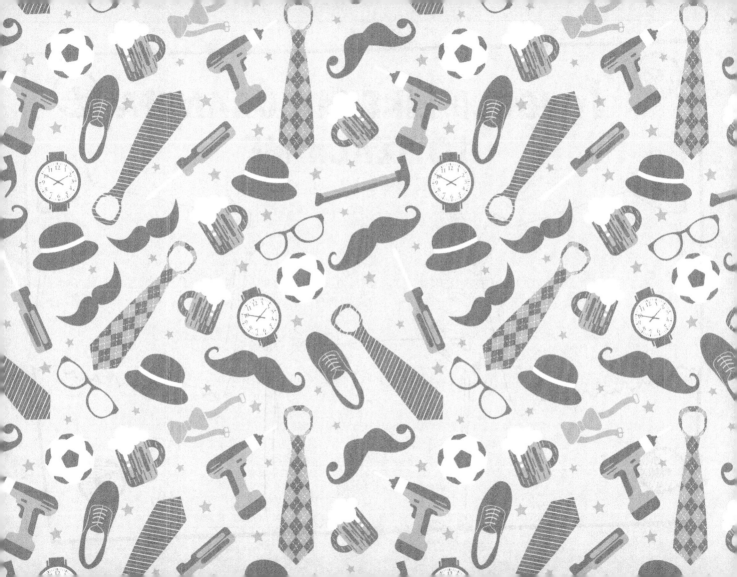

THE PERFECT DAY FOR MY GRANDPA iS

_____

THAT'S WHEN HE HAS PLENTY OF TiME TO

_____

My favorite photo with my Grandpa

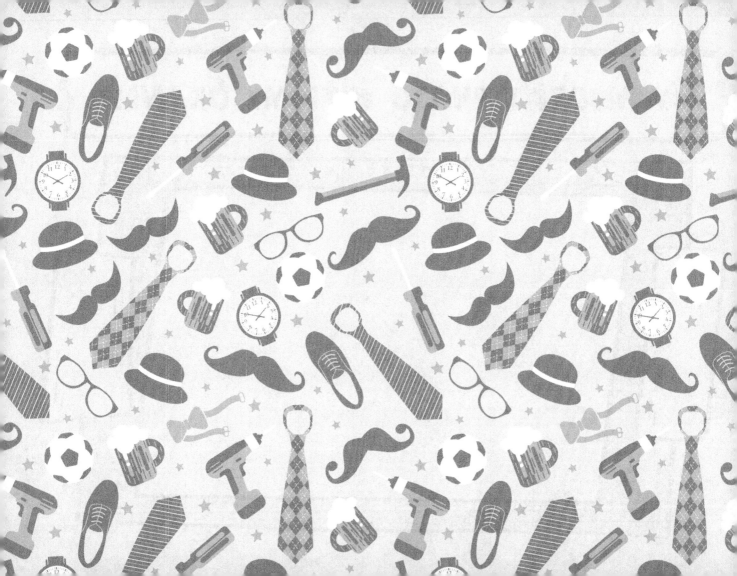

MY GRANDPA OFTEN TAKES ME TO

_____

I REALLY LIKE WHEN WE GO
THERE BECAUSE WE CAN

_____

GRANDPA'S GREATEST STRENGTHS ARE:

_____

_____

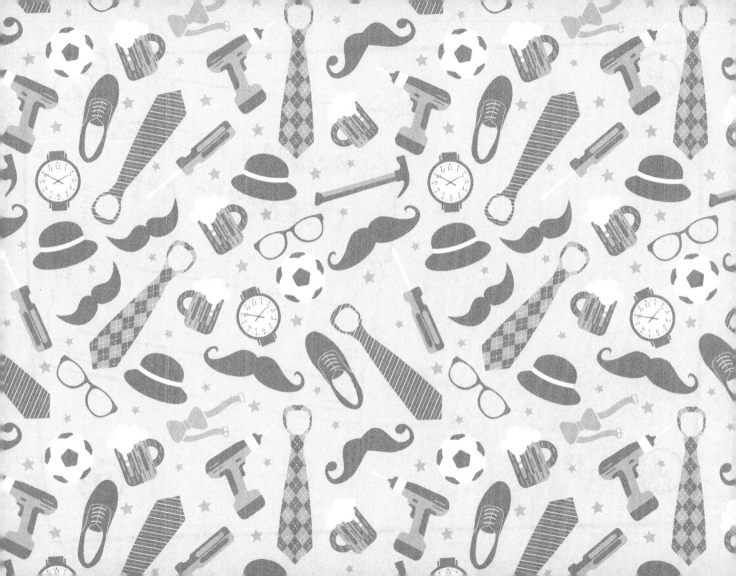

SUPER HERO

MY GRANDPA DEFINITELY HAS TO BE A SUPERHERO, HIS NICKNAME IS

HIS SUPERPOWER IS

SUPER HERO

MY GRANDPA'S BIGGEST DREAM

_____

_____

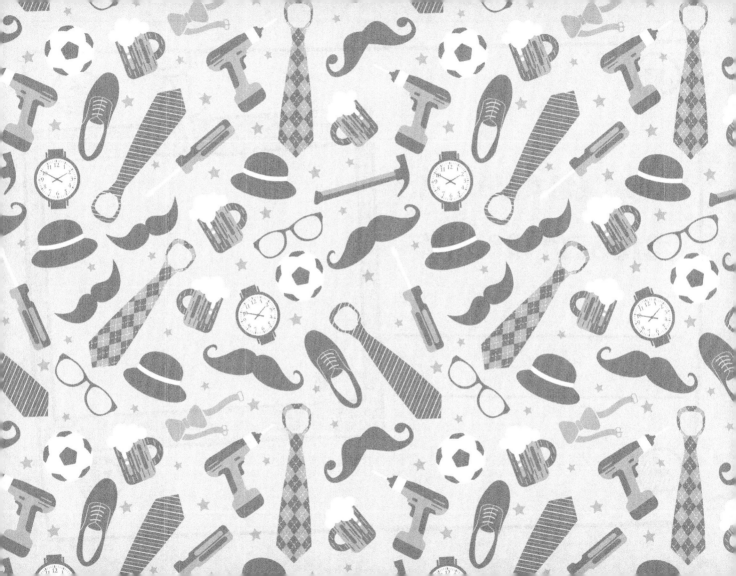

I AM MOST THANKFUL TO MY GRANDPA FOR

1. _____

2. _____

3. _____

THE BEST GIFT I EVER GOT FROM MY GRANDPA

_____

_____

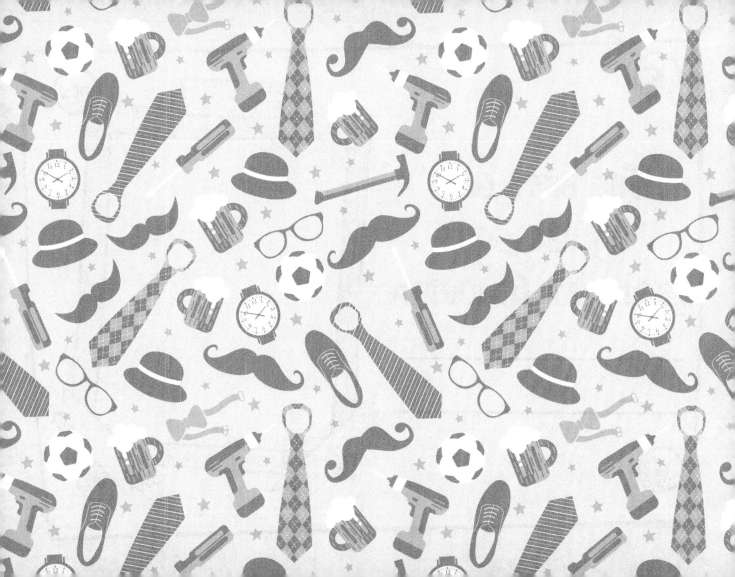

My Grandpa is happy when

_____

My Grandpa's favorite things are

_____

THE FIRST MEMORIES I HAVE WITH MY GRANDPA

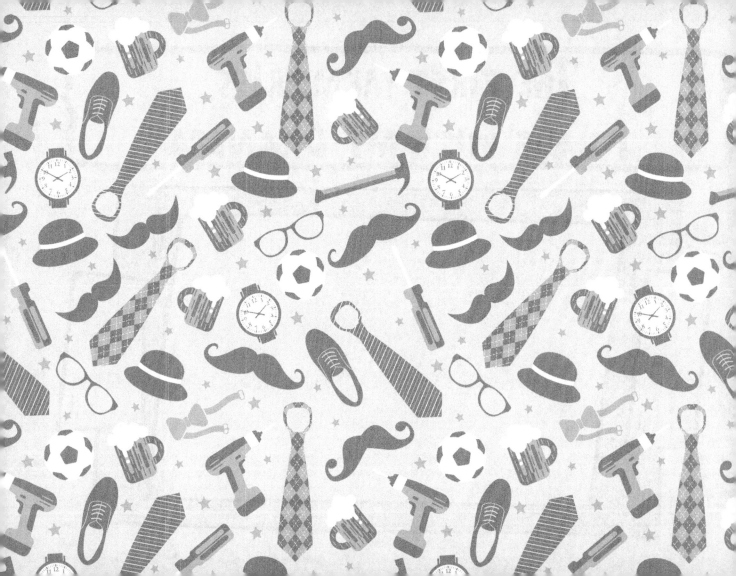

MOVIE TIME

My Grandpa and I really enjoy

watching _____

It's _____ and it

makes all the time

_____

GRANDPA AND I HAVE YET TO VISIT PLACES LIKE:

1._____

2._____

3._____

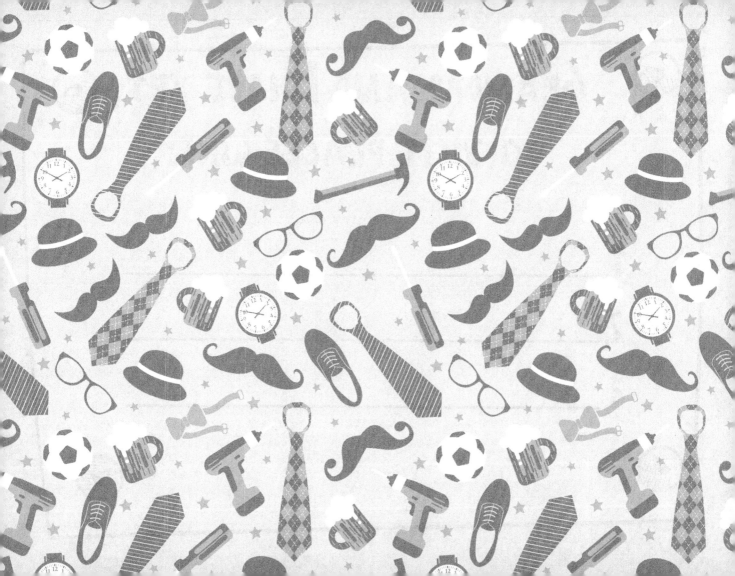

OUR FAVORITE GAMES ARE

_____

_____

BUT WE LIKE THE MOST
OF THESE

_____

I admire my Grandpa for

_____

_____

_____

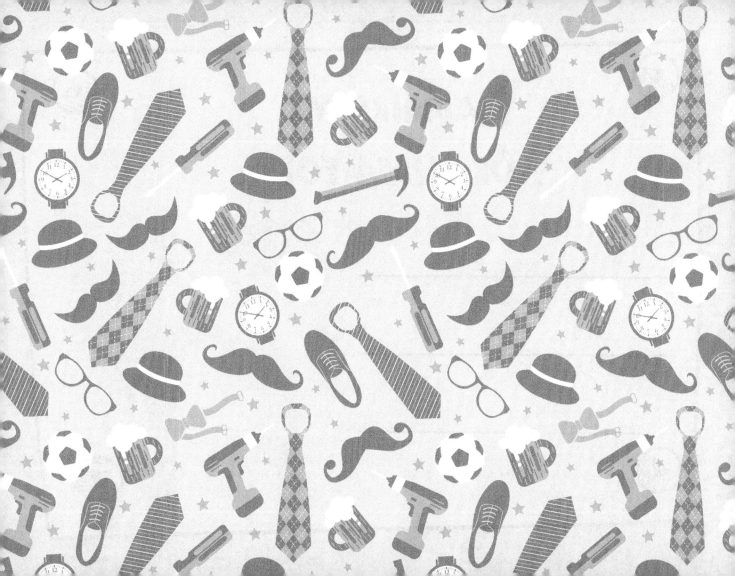

THE THINGS THAT MOST DESCRIBE MY GRANDPA

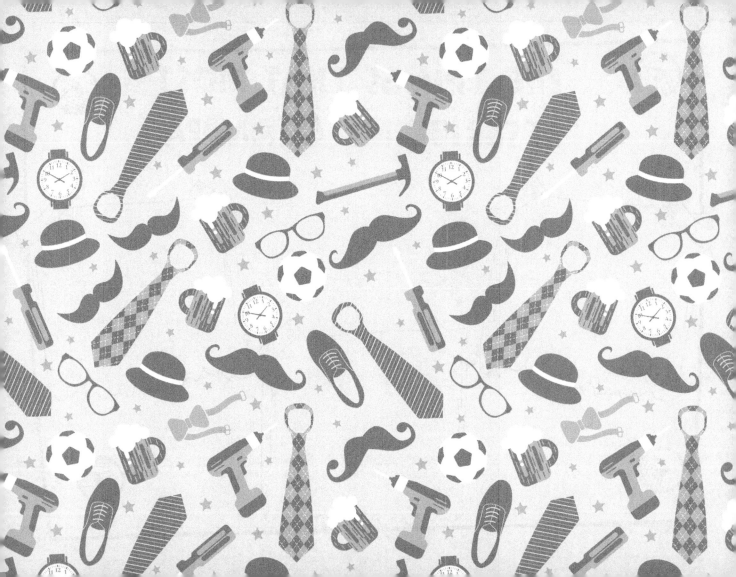

GRANDPA i WROTE A SPECIAL MESSAGES FOR YOU

 I CAN HAVE A LOT OF TOYS,
MEET COOL FRIENDS, BUT
I CAN ONLY HAVE

ONE SPECIAL GRANDPA

 I LOVE YOU GRANDPA

Made in the USA
Monee, IL
14 June 2022